D1087582

Can You Find These Flowers?

Carmen Bredeson and
Lindsey Cousins

Enslow Elementary
an imprint of

Enslow Publishers, Inc.
40 Industrial Road
Box 398
Berkeley Heights, NJ 07922
USA
http://www.enslow.com

Enslow Elementary, an imprint of Enslow Publishers, Inc.
Enslow Elementary® is a registered trademark of Enslow Publishers, Inc.

Library of Congress Cataloging-in-Publication Data

Bredeson, Carmen.

Can you find these flowers? / Carmen Bredeson and Lindsey Cousins.
p. cm. — (All about nature)
Includes index.
Summary: "Learn about wildflowers such as: goldenrod, dandelions, black-eyed susans, and forget-me-nots"—Provided by publisher.
ISBN 978-0-7660-3976-6
1. Wild flowers—Identification—Juvenile literature. I. Cousins, Lindsey. II. Title.
QK85.5.B74 2012
582.13—dc23
2011014457

Future editions:
Paperback ISBN 978-1-4644-0067-4
ePUB ISBN 978-1-4645-0974-2
PDF ISBN 978-1-4646-0974-9

Printed in China

012012 Leo Paper Group, Heshan City, Guangdong, China

10 9 8 7 6 5 4 3 2 1

To Our Readers: We have done our best to make sure all Internet Addresses in this book were active and appropriate when we went to press. However, the author and the publisher have no control over and assume no liability for the material available on those Internet sites or on other Web sites they may link to. Any comments or suggestions can be sent by e-mail to comments@enslow.com or to the address on the back cover.

Photo Credits: © 2011 Photos.com, a division of Getty Images. All rights reserved., pp. 8, 11, 12, 14, 15, 18, 19, 22; Jane Katirgis, p. 1; Shutterstock.com, pp. 3, 4, 6, 7, 9, 10, 13, 16, 17, 20, 21, 23.

Cover Photo: Shutterstock.com

Note to Parents and Teachers

Help pre-readers get a jump start on reading. These lively stories introduce simple concepts with repetition of words and short simple sentences. Photos and illustrations fill the pages with color and effectively enhance the text. Free Educator Guides are available for this series at www.enslow.com. Search for the *All About Nature* series name.

Contents

Words to Know

nectar (NEK tur)— The sweet juice in a flower.

petal (PEH tuhl)

stem (STEM)

Parts of a Plant

Finding Flowers

Flowers grow in the ground.

You may see them in fields.

You may see them along roads.

Flowers come in many colors.

Look outside.

Can you find some of the flowers in this book?

Dandelion

Dandelion flowers are yellow.

Then the flowers dry up.

The seeds are white.

They look like a fluffy ball.

Blow on the seeds.

Watch them fly!

Look at the red line.

It shows how tall the plant grows.

The person is about your size.

Black-Eyed Susan

These flowers

have yellow *petals*.

The middle is called the eye.

Are the eyes really black?

No, they are dark brown.

Clover

Clover plants

grow low in the grass.

The flowers can be red or white.

They can be purple or yellow.

Clover smells sweet.

Goldenrod

Goldenrods are very tall plants. The flowers are tiny. But they grow close together. The *stems* are very long. You can see big fields of goldenrod.

Thistle

Thistle flowers start

as thorny green balls.

Then fluffy petals

open on top.

They can be pink, purple, or yellow.

The stems have sharp points.

Be careful!

Wood Sorrel

Look at this plant's leaves. They are in the shape of a heart. The flowers grow on thin stems. They are yellow or white. Each flower has five petals.

Queen Anne's Lace

Little white flowers

grow in a bunch.

They look like white lace.

The flowers are on top

of long stems.

Wind blows the flowers

back and forth.

Butterfly Weed

These flowers are bright orange.

The leaves are long and thin.

Each little flower has

a lot of *nectar*.

Butterflies drink the

sweet juice.

Forget-Me-Not

Each flower has five blue petals.

The flowers smell

sweet at night.

Seeds grow on the stems.

Shake the stems.

Watch the seeds fall.

Read More

Helbrough, Emma. *How Flowers Grow*. London: Usborne, 2007.

Loves, June. *Flowers*. Philadelphia: Chelsea Club House, 2005.

Nelson, Tracy. *Growing Flowers*. Vero Beach, Fla.: Rourke Publishing, 2002.

Web Sites

National Geographic: Little Kids. *Planting Seeds*. <http://kidsblogs.nationalgeographic.com/littlekids/plant-seeds.html>

U.S. Forest Service. *Celebrating Wildflowers*. <http://www.fs.fed.us/wildflowers/kids>

Index

Guided Reading Level: E
Guided Reading Leveling System is based on the guidelines recommended by Fountas and Pinnell.

Word Count: 261